JERRY BRONDFIELD

SCHOLASTIC BOOK SERVICES
New York Toronto London Auckland Sydney Tokyo

ISBN 0-590-05725-1

Copyright © 1979 by Scholastic Magazines, Inc. All rights reserved. Published by Scholastic Book Services, a division of Scholastic Magazines, Inc.

12 11 10 9 8 7 6 5 4 3 2 1   9   9/7 0 1 2 3 4/8

Printed in the U. S. A.   01

CONTENTS

ALL-PRO
OFFENSE
1978

WR: **Lynn Swann,** Pittsburgh Steelers
WR: **Wesley Walker,** New York Jets
TE: **Dave Casper,** Oakland Raiders
 T: **Leon Gray,** New England Patriots
 T: **Dan Dierdorf,** St. Louis Cardinals
 G: **Joe DeLamielleure,** Buffalo Bills
 G: **John Hannah,** New England Patriots
 C: **Mike Webster,** Pittsburgh Steelers
 Q: **Terry Bradshaw,** Pittsburgh Steelers
RB: **Earl Campbell,** Houston Oilers
RB: **Walter Payton,** Chicago Bears

1

Wide Receiver
LYNN SWANN
6-0, 180
PITTSBURGH STEELERS

If Lynn Swann hadn't been a football player, he could have been a world-famous ballet dancer. The truth is that the Steelers' super receiver is the most graceful performer in the NFL. No one can match his combination of speed, leaping ability, timing, body control, and sure hands.

Swann catches 'em high, wide, low, off to either side, and points north, south, east, and west. He runs pass patterns the way they're designed in the playbook. And often, when a play breaks down and his QB is being pressured too much, Swann will come up with a pattern of his own. Anything to get near that ball.

The Steelers made him a first-round draft pick after he'd made lots of headlines as All-America at Southern California. He was a Pittsburgh starter from the first step he took on the practice field in camp.

It was only a matter of time before the experts would realize he was an All-Pro. Last season he caught 61 passes for 880 yards and 11 touchdowns. Hooking up with QB Terry Bradshaw, Swann was one of the most important factors in the Steelers' great offense — and their Super Bowl championship.

When his football days are over (not for many years) he'll probably go into TV and radio work.

Wide Receiver
WESLEY WALKER
6-0, 172
NEW YORK JETS

If you use "promising" to describe Wesley Walker's rookie season in 1977, then you have to use "spectacular" for his first year as a vet in 1978. Never has a second-year man led the NFL in yards gained per catch, which is what the Jets' swift receiver did with a 24.4 yard mark. Simple math tells you that's the equivalent of two first downs for every completion. By the way, his 1,169 total yards also led the NFL.

There's another way to describe Walker. He can adapt. He had to adapt to two QBs with the Jets — Richard Todd and Matt Robinson. He worked smoothly with both, learning to adjust to the way they released the ball as well as the "hardness" or "softness" of the ball they threw.

Walker's biggest asset is his overall speed and acceleration. He has the gift of shifting gears on defending backs. He gets behind them before they realize where he is or where he is going.

The Jets knew they were getting a super athlete when they drafted him from the University of California. He was the Golden Bears' first four-year, two-sport man in 40 years. As a track star, he ran a leg of Cal's sprint-relay team. In football, he set an NCAA record for career average pass reception of 25.7 yards per catch, which is just about the figures for his big season as a pro last year.

Tight End
DAVE CASPER
6-4, 230
OAKLAND RAIDERS

Looking for a name for Dave Casper? Try any of the following: Mr. Steady. Mr. Consistent. Mr. Spectacular. Mr. Do-Everything. Any one or all of them will do.

"There's just no one better at all phases of his job," says former Raider coach John Madden. "If he's just called upon to block, he explodes out of there and knocks his man right out of the play. If the assignment calls for him to block his man first, and then run his pass route, he does it, bang-bang. He hits, releases off his man, and next thing you know he's slipping into the seams of the zone coverage. He gets open as slick as any tight end I've seen."

There's one other thing. Or two. Casper has great hands for the ball. And once he tucks it away, he's like a bull elephant. The secondary has to converge on him mighty fast, because it usually takes two to bring him down.

He doesn't have great speed, but he doesn't waste his moves. He knows where he's going at all times and when he and the ball arrive there together, the Raider drive is another 10 or 15 yards closer to the goal line. His 62 catches for 852 yards and nine touchdowns gave him the best all-around stats for the year among tight ends.

Offensive Tackle
LEON GRAY
6-3, 260
NEW ENGLAND PATRIOTS

When Leon Gray played the trumpet in his Mississippi high school band, he was excused from 10 band appearances each year. Those were the Friday nights he played tackle for the football team. Gray took his football skills to Jackson State College, Mississippi, but left his trumpet home. It may have been music's loss, but it sure was football's gain.

Gray started for four years at Jackson and became a third-round draft choice by the Miami Dolphins. The Dolphins soon made a mistake. They cut him in camp and put him out for waivers. The Patriots grabbed him right after the final cut.

Gray started the last eight games of the year for the Patriots as a rookie. He was definitely one of the future lineman stars of the season.

Soon Gray became known for his pass-blocking abilities. He was already a powerful blocker on running plays. Throughout the NFL, the defenses knew it wasn't going to be easy getting through to sack Steve Grogan, the Patriots' quarterback. Mostly because of Gray's protection, Grogan has been sacked very few times the last couple of seasons.

"He's my life insurance," beams Grogan. "He helps give me the confidence to stay an extra split-second in the pocket. Often it's the difference between a completion, an incompletion, or an interception." Or in getting the QB's head knocked off.

9

Offensive Tackle
DAN DIERDORF
6-2, 280
ST. LOUIS CARDINALS

Even if the St. Louis Cardinals *never* made the playoffs, they'd always have one distinction: Dan Dierdorf. Until old age catches up with him, he'll probably be an automatic All-Pro choice.

Do you need just one yard for a first down to keep your drive going? Simple. Just call the play over Dierdorf's tackle position and you're on your way. When that situation arises for the St. Louis Cardinals, enemy defenses brace for "Big Danny's" charge. More often than not, it doesn't do much good.

It has been happening for several years. Finally, four years ago, the experts sat up and said: "Hey, it's time this guy was All-Pro!" So now Dierdorf has made it four straight years.

There are two things an offensive tackle must do to survive in the NFL, and Dierdorf does both. He's a great blocker on running plays and provides tight protection for his quarterback on passing plays.

Dierdorf, who was All-America at Michigan, is a big reason why Jim Hart, the Cardinals' QB, is usually sacked fewer times by opposing linemen each season than any QB in the league. "It gives me more confidence," says Hart, "and more time to get my passes off, knowing that Dan is out there in front of me, keeping those big ends from getting to me."

Dierdorf is also a tough, durable player who has not missed a game with an injury in the last seven years. He has excellent balance and is never out of position when he makes his block. The perfect offensive tackle.

11

Offensive Guard

JOE
DeLAMIELLEURE

6-3, 245
BUFFALO BILLS

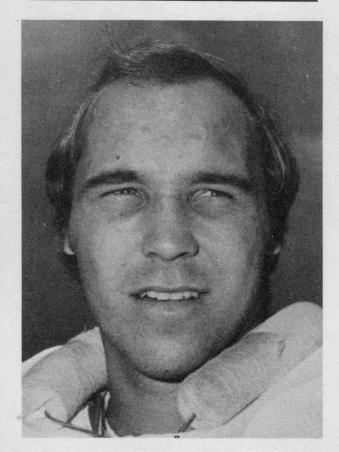

When the Buffalo coaches draw up the X's and O's on the blackboard, they tap the diagram and say to Joe DeLamielleure: "That's your man, Joe, get him!"

No problem. Joe D. always get his man.

When he was at Michigan State, he majored in criminal justice. "I wish he'd have gone into crime-busting instead of football," said an NFL linebacker. "When he comes out to lead interference, you can just see that steely glint in his eye as he concentrates on getting his man. And he nearly always does."

A first-round draft choice in 1973, DeLamielleure became an immediate starter for the Bills and made the All-Rookie team. It took him only two years to make the jump to All-Pro, and he's been a repeater ever since. But by the way he leads interference and drops back for pass protection, everyone had agreed he'd make it soon. He's also a ferocious straight-ahead blocker on running plays. "I love to run behind Joe," says rookie running star Terry Miller. "He's the kind of blocker a ball carrier should remember in his will."

DeLamielleure made the All–Big-Ten team in college three times, and topped it off as an All-America in his senior year. This is his fourth straight year as an All-Pro and, barring injury, he should make it five and six and seven and so on!

Joe has one more distinction going for him. He has one of the toughest names to spell in the entire NFL. If you don't believe it, take another look.

Offensive Guard
JOHN HANNAH
6-2, 265
NEW ENGLAND PATRIOTS

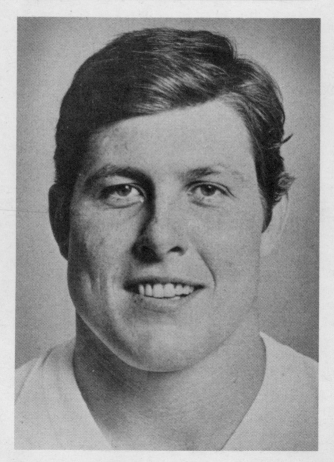

John Hannah felt insulted. He'd made All-Pro in 1976, but in 1977 the experts left him off the honor team. So last year, young Mister Hannah set out to prove they'd made a mistake — and to reclaim what was rightfully his.

He claimed it, all right! He did it by blasting holes the size of the Grand Canyon in NFL defensive lines. And one result was a play-off berth for the Patriots.

A lot of the ground-gaining came over Hannah's position, where he was a tremendous straight-ahead blocker. But Hannah carried out his other chores equally well. He was super at pulling out to block on wide plays, and he gave QB Steve Grogan excellent protection on passes.

Some people thought Hannah would have trouble in the pros, after starring at Alabama. Because Alabama used a wishbone offense, Hannah did all his blocking straight ahead. What would happen when he had to do so many different things in the pros? But 'Bama coach Bear Bryant said Hannah was the best lineman he'd ever had. "Don't worry about ol' Ham Hocks (Hannah's nickname)," said Bryant. "He'll do it all."

Bryant was right, of course. Hannah became a starter as a rookie and made the All-Rookie team after being drafted on the first round in 1973. Except for one game in his first season, he's started every game for the Patriots since then. Look for more All-Pro years for "ol' Ham Hocks."

Center
MIKE WEBSTER
6-½, 250
PITTSBURGH STEELERS

The Steelers didn't select Mike Webster until the sixth round of the draft a few years ago—which isn't very high. But the Steelers' coaches had him figured for two positions: guard or center. That way he had two chances. Actually he made good at both. He was an All-Rookie choice at center, but a year later, in 1976, he split the season at both posts. The following season he became the Steelers' center — for good. And better than good is the way to describe the former Wisconsin star.

He handles all snaps, not just to the quarterback but the longer ones for punts and place-kicks. Many centers can't do that. And when getting it into QB Terry Bradshaw's hands, he's a master of split-second timing. It's the best exchange in the NFL.

After the snap, Webster blocks with great ferocity and quickness. Even when the defense plays a man right over him, he isn't afraid of the slap to the head which centers must expect. He also has two other talents. He has the quick feet needed when a center drops back to give his QB pass protection. And on punts, after snapping the ball, he's one of the first downfield to close in on the punt returner. What it adds up to is All-Pro performance without weakness.

TERRY BRADSHAW
6-3, 215
PITTSBURGH STEELERS

You saw his sensational performance in the 1979 Super Bowl when he led the Steelers to a victory over Dallas, right? You saw his Super Bowl record of four touchdown passes and more than 300 yards in the air.

And maybe you wondered why it took Terry Bradshaw so long to become All-Pro.

For years he has played in the shadow of Bob Griese, Roger Staubach, and Ken Stabler when it came to naming the All-Pro QB. But Terry Bradshaw has finally emerged as football's best.

Bradshaw was the first player picked in the 1970 draft. He'd been All-America at Louisiana Tech, in the small-college division. He'd had super statistics, and the Steelers saw him as a rookie starter. He had the arm and the strength, but in that first year he led the NFL in interceptions, with 24. Not a pleasant record to hold.

He got better. In 1974–75 he became the youngest QB to lead his team to two straight NFL championships since Johnny Unitas did it for Baltimore in 1958–59. It looked as though Terry Bradshaw had arrived. But injuries set him back in 1976 and 1977. In fact, in 1977, he played the last 10 games of the season with a hard cast protecting a fractured bone in his left wrist.

Last year he was healthy again and the Steelers rolled. Much of their movement came from Bradshaw's 2,915 yards on 368 attempts, 207 completions, and 28 touchdowns. And that was nice icing on his cake in the Super Bowl, wasn't it?

And something many fans overlook is the fact that he's a great runner when he has to be. He's one of the Steelers' all-time leading rushers with a great 5.8 average and 27 TDs over the last eight seasons.

Running Back

EARL CAMPBELL

5-11, 224

HOUSTON OILERS

Listen to Dwight White of the Steelers: "Earl Campbell is almost illegal. When he hits that hole it's like a door slamming." And to the Steelers' Donnie Shell: "Earl Campbell is a Larry Csonka and O.J. Simpson combined." Some of the things other players say about the Oilers' rookie aren't printable.

Any way you look at it, Earl Campbell is the most exciting newcomer to the NFL in years. A unanimous All-America at the University of Texas, the Heisman winner was the Oilers' first draft pick (surprise! surprise!) after rushing for 4,444 yards as a Longhorn. Oh, he was super, all right, but would he bring all that talent to the pros? He brought it — and it was the reason the Oilers made the play-offs for the first time in their history.

Moving like a runaway freight train, Campbell used his brute power and great speed to run around tacklers or run over them if he had to. Often he would be hit by three or four people, but would break the tackles and continue on for four, five, or ten yards more. Defensive backs found his speed deceptive. He would be into the secondary before they were set to hit him. And often it would be too late.

Campbell's 1,450 yards for the year put him into a very select circle of only a half dozen runners in the history of the NFL who rushed for more than 1,000 yards as rookies. Already Campbell is being hailed as the man to break the legendary Jim Brown's lifetime mark of 12,312 yards.

Running Back
WALTER PAYTON
5-11, 204
CHICAGO BEARS

Question: If Walter Payton had an offensive line in front of him as good as the Miami Dolphins or Oakland Raiders, how many yards would he gain in a year? According to an NFL coach: "They'd measure it in miles, not yards."

With the Chicago Bears' not-so-good line working for him last year, Payton still led the National Conference in rushing with 1,395 yards and 11 TDs. If he ever gets the blocking, he's a cinch for 2,000 yards some year, enough to break O.J. Simpson's mark of 2,003. He almost did it in 1977 with 1,852.

Payton, from Jackson State, had a good break-in year as a rookie in 1975. Not sensational, but he showed the moves that would get him to the top.

"It isn't just his speed," says one NFL coach, "it's his blinding quickness. A lot of guys can stop on a dime, but how many can be off, full speed, on their first step?"

And a veteran NFL defensive back says: "He seems to come at you from all directions. I swear, he doesn't know himself which way he's going to cut."

His favorite maneuver looks like a broken play. He'll sweep right, see that he's cut off, and will stop and bolt all the way back to the left side. There won't be a blocker with him, but somehow he'll slice free for big yardage.

"The name of the game is confidence," says Payton. "I told them when I came up that I'd make it. Some people didn't listen because I wasn't all that big."

They're listening now, Walter.

ALL-PRO DEFENSE 1978

  E: **Jack Youngblood,** Los Angeles Rams
  E: **Al Baker,** Detroit Lions
  T: **Randy White,** Dallas Cowboys
  T: **Louie Kelcher,** San Diego Chargers
LB: **Randy Gradishar,** Denver Broncos
LB: **Jack Ham,** Pittsburgh Steelers
LB: **Robert Brazile,** Houston Oilers
CB: **Willie Buchanon,** ~~Green Bay Packers~~
CB: **Louis Wright,** Denver Broncos
FS: **Cliff Harris,** Dallas Cowboys
SS: **Charlie Waters,** Dallas Cowboys

Defensive End
JACK YOUNGBLOOD
6-4, 242
LOS ANGELES RAMS

Jack Youngblood has been named to the Pro-Bowl team six straight years. For much of that time, Rams fans have been screaming that Youngblood has been getting gypped: he should be All-Pro, as well.

Okay, all you Angelinos, here he is — Jack Youngblood, All-Pro. And last year, at least, there wasn't another defensive end who could touch him. A first-round draft choice from the University of Florida, in 1971, where he was All-America, Youngblood was one of the big reasons the Rams' defense was one of the most feared in the league. He sacks quarterbacks, and when he just misses a sack, he puts unholy pressure on them.

He rarely gets fully blocked out of the play, and he terrorizes the ball carriers. Nobody can recall the last time he failed to contain a sweep. The guy kicking extra points against the Rams usually has half an eye on the monster making a rush at him from the corner. What we're talking about is the *complete* defensive end, right?

During the off-season, Youngblood works for a bank credit-card company. But nobody gets more credit than Jack Youngblood among the NFL's defensive ends.

Defensive End
AL BAKER
6-6, 240
DETROIT LIONS

"As much as I'd like to believe it myself, I'm not really the 'Incredible Hulk,'" says Al Baker. "A lot of people won't believe it, but I don't even turn green."

Well, that's the direct word from the most sensational rookie end to ever hit the NFL. Rookies don't often make All-Pro. It happens only in seasons when the moon is made of green cheese. Green as in Hulk. When the Lions drafted Baker from Colorado State, the coaches took a look at him in early drills and said, "Hey, this kid has a great chance to start." Three games into the regular season and the whole league knew Al Baker was something special.

"He's always playing at fever pitch," said one veteran NFL observer. Maybe that's why he made 23 quarterback sacks in 1978, a record for rookies, and the best in the NFL season. Blockers couldn't nail him because he was so strong and agile. (He was also a star basketball player at Colorado State.) Ball carriers couldn't run around him, and trying to run over him could prove fatal. He used his hands like a five-year veteran, and the best pass blockers in the NFL rarely knocked him off balance.

If there's anything else required of him, nobody has thought of it yet.

RANDY WHITE
6-4, 250
DALLAS COWBOYS

Randy White has been around, defensively, but now he has finally found a home. He was an All-America defensive end at Maryland, but when the Cowboys made him a first-round draft choice five years ago, they made him a linebacker. Why not? He was big, strong, and very agile. In fact, he was downright quick. And mean. And determined. And intense. And he liked to hit ball carriers. See what we mean?

But although he started some games his first two years, he also served as a back-up. Coach Tom Landry decided on a switch. Because of his quickness and great strength, White would also make a great pass rusher at tackle, where he could be used all the time.

So, Randy White, in 1977, went into his third defensive position. He took to the job immediately and had a great season.

But 1978 saw him developing into a superstar. Quarterbacks around the league were fleeing for their lives as White put the pressure on them. When he wasn't sacking them he was making them get rid of the ball before they really wanted to. Meanwhile, he was making his share of tackles. Blockers rarely made him take a backward step.

What Randy White had become was the perfect defensive tackle and a big reason for the Cowboys' march to the Super Bowl.

Defensive Tackle

LOUIE KELCHER

6-5, 282

SAN DIEGO CHARGERS

Louie Kelcher is BIG. He wears size 16EEEE shoes, which is about the size of the working end of a canoe paddle. With a straight face he tells people that when he was 12 years old, they hired him to stamp out forest fires. So much for Louie Kelcher's feet. He also stamps out ball carriers who try to run over his position.

This five-year veteran, who was a second-round draft choice after starring for Southern Methodist University, was an All-Rookie his first year. Everyone predicted the All-Pro honor that is now his.

Defensive tackles in the NFL have to be big, strong, quick, and tough-minded. Louie tried all those on and they all fit. When the enemy has a short yardage situation for a first down, they just about never (make that never) try for it over Kelcher's position. He leads his front four in tackles, quarterback sacks, and intimidating the ball carrier.

"Louie gets great pursuit angles," say his coaches. "So, he never wastes a split second or a step. He always knows where he's going, and where to meet the ball carrier. Blocking him is terribly difficult. He hand-fights his blockers with great fury. Once he starts a charge, he can't be turned away."

Nobody can think of anything else they'd want from a defensive tackle.

Linebacker

RANDY GRADISHAR

6-3, 233
DENVER BRONCOS

Wherever the ball is, that's where you'll find Randy Gradishar. "He has a weird knack of being there," says Denver's defensive chief, Joe Collier. "Whether it's a running back headed for a hole in the line, or an enemy receiver going out for a pass, good ol' Randy gets there first. He doesn't miss many tackles, and one reason is his trick of staying unblocked."

Put it all together and you know why Gradishar was named the NFL's Defensive Player of the Year.

Randy attracted all the pro scouts' attention as an All-America at Ohio State. Woody Hayes, the Buckeyes' former coach, tagged him as "...the best linebacker I've ever seen." He'd been a three-year starter for the Bucks and an All-America, but the Bronco coaches held their breath a bit. He'd had a complicated knee operation after his final college season and only time would tell if it was successful. Other clubs decided to pass him up. The Broncos gambled and grabbed him on the first round of the 1974 draft.

The knee held up. Gradishar got in a lot of playing time his rookie year and became a starter — and a star — in his second season. He has been the Broncos' leader in tackles the last three seasons.

Linebacker

JACK HAM
6-1, 225
PITTSBURGH STEELERS

"Jack Ham, on any play," says a veteran NFL scout, "is always *where* he's supposed to be, and *when* he's supposed to be. You can count on it as surely as the sun rises in the east."

And he could have added: "He's also doing what he's supposed to do to the ball carrier or pass receiver, which is laying a furious pair of hands on him."

If you took a poll of all NFL coaches, Jack Ham would no doubt be voted the greatest linebacker in football today. Because of Ham and a few others who come close to him in ability, linebackers have become some of the most glamorous players in the NFL.

Wayne Walker, who starred for the Detroit Lions and is now a TV sportcaster, says: "Linebackers are usually among the most intelligent players on your team. They have to be to make the many adjustments the position calls for. They have to defend against the run *and* the pass and be able to smell out which it's going to be when so many plays start out the same way. Then they've got to have the speed and mental agility to adjust. And all the while they're taking a beating from blockers while their attention is elsewhere."

That's Jack Ham. Ham was an All-America at Penn State in 1970. The Steelers made him their second-round draft pick in 1971 and he rewarded them by making the starting lineup as a rookie. He's not big as linebackers go — only 6-1 and 225 pounds — but he makes up for it in intelligence, quickness, and alertness.

Linebacker

ROBERT BRAZILE

6-4, 238

HOUSTON OILERS

In 1975, Robert Brazile was not only a unanimous NFL All-Rookie but also was named Defensive Rookie of the Year. All the experts said that if they had to pick one newcomer who was a cinch to become a future All-Pro, they'd have to pick Brazile. With that kind of start, Brazile decided not to let anybody down. Especially himself.

An All-America at Jackson State, Mississippi, Brazile was a first-round draft pick by the Oilers. There were a few critics who said Brazile was too tall, at 6-4, for a linebacker. Guys that tall weren't able to react and change direction as nimbly as shorter players. The ideal linebacker, they said, was 6-2. Brazile soon made a lot of people think 6-4 was ideal.

Not only was he a deadly tackler, but he had the upper body strength which linebackers need to ward off blockers. And, as for quick reactions, Brazile's 4.6 speed for 40 yards was the fastest for any linebacker in the NFL. Seldom is he faked out on a play. Rarely is he blocked out. Never does he fail to stop a runner once he gets his hands on him. He's been chosen All-Pro three times since he broke in. Nobody is saying there'll never be a fourth time.

Cornerback
WILLIE BUCHANON*
6-0, 190
GREEN BAY PACKERS

Willie Buchanon is a man of great extremes. On one hand he is a tender man who loves plants and has more than 40 in his apartment. On the other, he loves to hit people — only from his defensive backfield position, of course.

Buchanon is also a football player who overcame great odds to rise to the top. A first-round draft choice from San Diego State, California, he nailed down a starting job the first game of his rookie season in 1972. It looked as though he had a great future ahead of him. A year later, disaster struck. He broke his leg in a game against the Rams. He worried about it for the next six months. Would he be able to come back? Yes, his leg healed, and he had a fine year in 1974. But in 1975, in the second game against Denver, he fractured the same leg in a different place. Again he was out for the rest of the season, and had to worry about the future.

Willie was lucky. This break healed perfectly, too. In 1976 and 1977 he led the Packer secondary in tackles. Ball carriers around the NFL said he was one of the hardest hitters in the league. Last year, there was no question of Willie Buchanon's all-around play. His pass defense was superb; his fierce play against the run was legendary. Willie was entitled to his All-Pro honors.

*Has since been traded to the San Diego Chargers

Cornerback
LOUIS WRIGHT
6-2, 195
DENVER BRONCOS

It isn't enough to just have great speed and hitting ability as a cornerback. You also have to have great reflexes and instincts. Rich McCabe, coach of the Broncos' defensive backs, says Louie Wright has some of the fastest reflexes in the NFL. "I've never seen a defensive back who can recover so quickly when what looks like a run turns into a pass, or vice versa. For Louie there isn't a split second of lost motion when he has to make the switch.

"His great reflexes and instincts show up, too, when a pass receiver tries to burn him with a quick cut on a pass route. He thinks he's shaken Louie, but Louie doesn't get lost very easily. I always have confidence that Louie will recover to bat down the ball or intercept it."

Wright, a star collegian at Long Beach State, California, is also the Broncos' fastest player with a sizzling 4.4 for 40 yards. In college he ran the 100 in 9.6 and was an All-Coast selection. The Broncos didn't wait very long to grab him in the draft. He was only the second player in Denver history to be snatched up as a first-round choice. And now that he's made All-Pro for the first time, mark him down as a sure repeater.

Free Safety
CLIFF HARRIS
6-1, 190
DALLAS COWBOYS

Someone once said that Cliff Harris is the only bald (well, almost bald) All-Pro safety in NFL history. But who needs hair when you can do what he does?

First of all, you'd have to say Cliff Harris made All-Pro the hard way. He played for Ouachita (pronounced WASH-e-taw) Baptist University in Arkadelphia, Arkansas. Not many football fans have heard of Ouachita Baptist and not many pro scouts know the airline schedules to Arkadelphia. So Harris had no pro teams searching him out. But he asked the Cowboys for a chance in 1970 and signed on as a free agent. From now on the Cowboys will keep Ouachita in mind.

Harris, a tremendous hitter, became an instant starter. But then he was called into military service and had to begin all over again when he came back. Same story. Regained his starting job immediately.

Harris is a master at psyching the receivers he has to cover. "I love to play a mental game with them," he says. "If you step in front of a receiver and make an interception, he'll just be a little upset. But if you blast him and really spin his helmet around and ring his bell, he'll lose some of his concentration for the ball.

"Sometimes," he continues, "I even talk to them. I ask them, 'Is it worth it?' It sinks in and makes my job a bit easier."

No matter whether he plays a physical or mental game, Harris can do it all. The only time he doesn't have football on his mind is in the summer when he works on getting his Master's Degree in environmental biology. He doesn't like things polluting the air. Including footballs.

Strong Safety

CHARLIE WATERS

6-2, 198
DALLAS COWBOYS

For the second straight year, the Cowboys did what no NFL team ever did before — placed both their safeties on All-Pro.

The strong safety doesn't have the freedom to roam as much as the free safety; he must concern himself with the enemy's tight end. And because tight ends are so big, the strong safety has to be extra tough.

Charlie Waters was simply sensational in the job he did last year. "I've never seen an athlete concentrate the way he did," said Dallas coach Tom Landry. "I guess he decided that he wanted to be an All-Pro repeater. I can't recall a safety hitting as hard as he did, and I can't remember the last mistake he made in his coverage." Other coaches and the sports writers felt that way, too.

Waters never dreamed 10 years ago that he'd ever play safety in the NFL. He'd divided his time at Clemson University as a quarterback and wide receiver. His QB experience came in handy when Dallas made him a third-round draft choice and moved him into the secondary. He knew what passing and pass routes were all about. Charlie fit in perfectly with his new chores and made the starting lineup as a rookie. "I don't just want to be the best at my job in the eyes of the fans and writers," he says. "I want to be the best in my own eyes."

ALL-ROOKIE OFFENSE 1978

WR: **John Jefferson**, San Diego Chargers
WR: **James Lofton**, Green Bay Packers
TE: **Ozzie Newsome**, Cleveland Browns
 T: **Mike Kenn**, Atlanta Falcons
 T: **Chris Ward**, New York Jets
 G: **Walter Downing**, San Francisco 49ers
 G: **Homer Elias**, Detroit Lions
 C: **Blair Bush**, Cincinnati Bengals
 Q: **Doug Williams**, Tampa Bay Buccaneers
RB: **Terry Miller**, Buffalo Bills
RB: **Earl Campbell**, Houston Oilers

Wide Receiver
JOHN JEFFERSON
6-1, 184
SAN DIEGO CHARGERS

Take a look at these stats! In his rookie year last season, John Jefferson caught 56 passes for 1,001 yards and 13 touchdowns. He led the whole NFL in TDs and was fourth in yardage. . . . The league's leading rookie receiver was the first NFL newcomer to gain at least 1,000 yards receiving in almost 10 years (since the Eagles' Harold Jackson in 1969). The Chargers drafted him after he'd caught 175 passes for 2,824 yards at Arizona State.... They checked the films, saw his blazing speed and the nifty way he ran pass routes, and all the coaches whistled at once.... There was no doubt in anyone's mind that Jefferson would make the starting team from game one.... He did, of course, and is on his way to scaring most of the NFL's defensive backs out of their wits — and their shoes, too!

There's no great surprise here. Everyone knew that Jim Lofton was going to make it quick and make it big in the NFL.... Stanford University always comes up with terrific receivers and it was

Lofton's turn.... One of the nation's finest long-jumpers, he had the great spring, leaping ability, and sure hands...."Perfect tools of the trade," said the Packer coaches. "And watch him go up in a crowd and accelerate once he has that leather in his hands." Then they turned him loose as a rookie starter in the NFL and Lofton made their predictions look good.... Even the veteran cornerbacks and safeties had trouble flagging him down. In his first year he reminded everyone of the Steelers' fabulous Lynn Swann.... The stats held up for him, too, as he broke into the National Conference's top 20 with 46 receptions and six TDs.

OZZIE NEWSOME
6-2, 225
CLEVELAND BROWNS

Coach Bear Bryant of Alabama called him "the best receiver we've ever had." Not a bad recommendation, and the Cleveland Browns bought it.... Newsome's four-year mark at 'Bama was 102 receptions for 2,070 yards and a brilliant 20.3 yards-per-catch average.... The word for that is WOW! But the key to Newsome's success as a pro would be whether he could block those mountainous pro defensive tackles and ends.... After all, 225 isn't big weight for a pro tight end.... But Ozz put a lot of 'em back on their heels with his fierce charge — and many of 'em flat on the ground. "I enjoy blocking," he says. "I enjoy making a key block that leads to a first down or touchdown." Well, maybe that's the way it is, and maybe not.... But if the Browns' super prospect likes it that way — good luck, Ozzie!

Offensive Tackle
MIKE KENN
6-6, 257
ATLANTA FALCONS

When the Falcons made Mike Kenn a first-round draft choice they knew he wasn't the flashy kind. He didn't say much and he wasn't colorful. But the Atlanta coaches studied his game films from Michigan and decided that what he did best was to get the job done — just about every play.

Kenn wasn't intimidated by the veteran defensive men in camp and he showed little respect for enemy linemen when he earned a starting role in the fall.... With half the season gone, the word was that the Falcon rookie had an explosive charge on running plays and was quickly learning how to set up pass protection for his QB.... "Natural ability," was the verdict of the critics. "And when this kid puts on 10 or 15 pounds he'll be an All-Pro candidate some day."

Offensive Tackle
CHRIS WARD
6-4, 265
NEW YORK JETS

Sure, he was a first-round draft choice and all that.... And his size, 6-4, 265, was impressive. So was his quickness off the ball.... But what about pass-blocking? As a two-time All-America at Ohio State, Chris Ward hadn't been called upon to provide a lot of pass protection. So, how quickly could he adjust to the pro game? Would he need a year to learn? Everyone found out in a hurry. Because that's the way Ward does things. Smart and coachable, he immediately showed he could do it all. He could blast straight ahead and downfield. He could drop back and save his QB's life. And he became a starter from day number one. Next stop on his honors course? For Chris Ward, make a reservation for All-Pro.... Say, in a couple of years at most.

Offensive Guard
WALTER DOWNING
6-3, 254
SAN FRANCISCO 49ERS

Although Walt Downing was an All-America center at Michigan, the 49ers coaches took a look at his blocking ability and his quickness and said, "Uh-uh, he goes to guard." In the camp, Walt proved the coaches right.... They liked that evil glint in his eye when he pulled out on trap plays, or led the interference on sweeps. Now, all they had to do was teach him some of the tricks of pass protection for the QB.... Downing was a good student, did his homework, and began his first pro season with a great desire to knock somebody's socks off.... Soon there were a lot of NFL defensive linemen and linebackers who had sock problems ....The prediction here is that in a couple of years, Walt Downing will be a candidate for All-Pro.

Offensive Guard
HOMER ELIAS
6-3, 260
DETROIT LIONS

They called him "Sugar Bear" when he starred at Tennessee State, but there was nothing sweet about him on the football field.... But there was a lot about him that went with the "Bear." The Detroit coaches didn't draft him until the fourth round, but in camp they thanked their lucky stars that nobody had drafted him earlier. Elias was the strongest rookie in sight.... He had great drive in his legs and hitting power in his shoulders.... Homer Elias was a starting guard for the Lions early in the regular season.... Rarely did he miss a blocking assignment, even on the NFL's best defensive linemen.... He could block straight ahead or pull out on a trap or sweep.... And as good as he is, he's going to get better.

Center
BLAIR BUSH
6-3, 254
CINCINNATI BENGALS

The Bengals draft-
ed Bush in the first
round and figured
the former University
of Washington star
would be a good
back-up for veteran
Bob Johnson. Bush
was more than that
and quickly earned
"varsity" status with the Bengals.... One
of the youngest players in the NFL (only 21
when he reported to camp), Bush caught
everyone's attention.... He had "quick
feet," which coaches like to see in a center
when he drops back for pass protection....
He was a straight-ahead strong blocker
and, as the season wore on, he showed his
talent as a long snapper on punts and
place-kicks.... Another thing he had was
courage.... Centers take a lot of punish-
ment around the head when they're over
the ball, but this young rookie hung in
there and made his attackers pay by put-
ting terrific blocks on them.

Quarterback
DOUG WILLIAMS
6-4, 214
TAMPA BAY BUCCANEERS

The Buccaneers had looked at him, live, in action, and stared, pop-eyed, at his stats. They were delighted at what they saw in both cases.... And they made Doug Williams their first choice in the draft. He was also the first QB picked in the whole NFL draft. And why not? He had the size. At Grambling College he set a major college record of most yards per completion at 18.2 His 38 touchdowns in 1977 is second best in college history.... He tossed a TD pass in every game he started (three years) except one. He brought his strong arm and poise into the NFL and was an immediate starter for the Bucs.... Halfway through the year, he broke his jaw and missed several games. But he'd served notice that he was for real, and would soon be hailed as one of the NFL's super QBs.

Running Back
TERRY MILLER
5-11, 192
BUFFALO BILLS

Terry Miller took a lot of joshing from teammates at Oklahoma State.... He had tender hamstring muscles, so, for protection, he wore a woman's long, stretch panty-girdle under his football pants....  Nobody joshed the results as Miller twice was an All-America running back and second to Earl Campbell in the 1977 Heisman voting.... As the Bills' first-round draft pick would he replace O.J. Simpson as a running threat...? Don't bet against it.... It was immediate stardom for Miller as he ran 1,060 yards in his rookie year.... Nobody ever said the Bills had a great offensive line in front of him, either, but everyone says Terry Miller has the speed, power, and zig-zag instincts to do much of it on his own.

EARL CAMPBELL

5-11, 224
HOUSTON OILERS

(See All-Pro)

ALL-ROOKIE DEFENSE 1978

- E: **Ross Browner,** Cincinnati Bengals
- E: **Al Baker,** Detroit Lions
- T: **Don Latimer,** Denver Broncos
- T: **Dee Hardison,** Buffalo Bills
- LB: **Reggie Wilkes,** Philadelphia Eagles
- LB: ~~**John Anderson,** Green Bay Packers~~
- LB: **Dan Bunz,** San Francisco 49ers
- CB: **Ron Johnson,** Pittsburgh Steelers
- CB: **Bobby Jackson,** New York Jets
- S: **Ken Greene,** St. Louis Cardinals
- S: **John Harris,** Seattle Seahawks

Defensive End
ROSS BROWNER
6-3, 262
CINCINNATI BENGALS

"He runs like a deer, he has great strength, he always knows where the ball is, and he has a high intensity." That's the praise sung by Bengal defensive-line coach, Chuck Studley.... It isn't exactly news.... Notre Dame opponents knew that for four years, while Browner was making All-America for two of them.... He won the Outland Trophy as Lineman of the Year in 1977.... Although Browner put on more than 40 pounds since high school, he has never lost any speed, and was a starter from his first day in camp. Even in his first year as a pro, he quickly showed the knack of sliding off the blockers and containing the ball carrier. And he'll be one of the best pass rushers in the NFL before he's through.

AL BAKER

6-6, 240
DETROIT LIONS

(See All-Pro)

Defensive Tackle
DON LATIMER
6-2, 260
DENVER BRONCOS

When the Broncos made Don Latimer a first-round draft choice, they tabbed him as a nose guard in Denver's 3-4 set up. The former Miami University (Florida) tackle had great speed and strength but, after all, he was only 6-2, and everyone knows that's not tall enough to play tackle in the NFL.... But when the Broncos saw they needed defensive tackles, the coaches said, "Heck, this guy doesn't have to be any taller. He's so quick and tough he'll just manhandle people in getting to the ball. So what if his upraised arms aren't high enough to bother the quarterback?" Well, Don Latimer bothered the QBs plenty.... He put them on his most-wanted list all season and became another star in the Broncos' galaxy.

DEE HARDISON
6-4, 268
BUFFALO BILLS

If the Bills were never in the race, don't blame any of it on Dee Hardison.... If everybody on the Bills played up to potential the way Hardison did, Buffalo could have had Super Bowl dreams. ...Hardison, an All-America defensive tackle at North Carolina State, was pegged as a defensive end when he reported to the Bills' camp, but the coaches saw his strength and pass-rush potential and moved him back to tackle.... Hardison was a starter almost from the beginning, and even the most experienced offensive linemen in the league had trouble moving him out.... He had such natural athletic ability that he became North Carolina State's star heavyweight wrestler even though he'd never wrestled in high school.

Linebacker
REGGIE WILKES
6-4, 227
PHILADELPHIA EAGLES

The Eagles had traded away their first two draft choices last year but they wasted no time picking Reggie Wilkes on their first available pick — the third round.... Wilkes was a gifted all-around  athlete who was also a basketball star in high school. A super linebacker at Georgia Tech, he was also a Dean's List student in biology, and may decide to study medicine some day.... There were a lot of low-keyed whistles in the Eagles camp when he showed his ability.... "Born to hit," said one defensive coach. "Head-hunting must be his hobby," said another.... Meanwhile, he was learning the pro tricks of the trade from a master alongside him: Bill Bergey, the Eagles' great linebacker.... By mid-season, the NFL knew Reggie Wilkes had arrived.

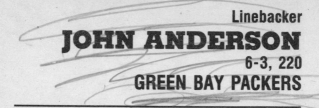

Linebacker
JOHN ANDERSON
6-3, 220
GREEN BAY PACKERS

Another of the Packers' young nifties, so watch the Pack in a couple of years.... At Michigan, Anderson was a defensive end, although called an "outside linebacker" by the Wolverines. But the Packers tabbed him as a linebacker, period, when he reported.... He was a great natural athlete with speed, great reflexes and reactions.... The ball never escaped his eye and it took him only a split second to read where the play was going.... The only question remaining was whether he had the hand and arm strength to fight off huge NFL blockers who like to take direct aim at linebackers....No problem. Anderson went into NFL action as though he was born to the idea....By the way, Anderson also has the "smarts," too. At Michigan, he was an Academic All-America.

66

Linebacker
DAN BUNZ
6-4, 230
SAN FRANCISCO 49ERS

What do you do with a guy who is 6-4, weighs 230, is a weight lifter, and can cover ground like an antelope? If you're a pro coach you make him a middle linebacker.... And that's just what the 49ers had in mind when they drafted Dan Bunz out of Long Beach (California) State on the first round.... As an All-Coast linebacker, he was in on 448 tackles in three years, which is strictly "whew!..." The 49ers figured he might be as effective in the pros if he could handle the slicker blocking assignments the pros throw at the defense.... No problem.... Bunz came to camp and started to stake out a claim to a starting job.... With his nose for the ball, he was rarely fooled, and was seldom blocked out of the play.... He carried the same habits into regular season play.

Cornerback
RON JOHNSON
5-10, 200
PITTSBURGH STEELERS

Ron Johnson went to Eastern Michigan University as a "walk-on." That means nobody thought him worthy of an athletic scholarship. He'd have to prove he could play before they'd award him a scholarship.... He proved it in his freshman season.... And by graduation, every pro team knew he could play defense in the NFL. The Steelers grabbed him in the first round of the draft and immediately knew they weren't wrong.... With his strength, quickness, and hitting ability Johnson laid "the force" on ball carriers and pass receivers.... He met runners at the line of scrimmage and hounded the pass catchers like a shadow.... Very aggressive and physical, he reminded a lot of experts of the Oakland Raiders' famed Jack Tatum when Tatum was a rookie. That means he's a bit of all right!

Cornerback
BOBBY JACKSON
5-9, 175
NEW YORK JETS

What's a little guy like this doing an All-Rookie thing in the NFL? Doing very well, thank you.... One of the toughest and most aggressive newcomers in years, Jackson played in his junior high band be-  cause the football coach said he was too small.... So Bobby Jackson went on to become an All-Georgia high school defensive back and honorable All-America at Florida State.... The Jets didn't pick him until the sixth round in the draft, but he made eyes pop in camp and became an immediate starter.... He played tough against the best receivers in the NFL with his tremendous speed and jumping ability, which he learned from hitchhiking rides on the back of garbage trucks while growing up in Georgia. Well, that's one way, but he doesn't think it a good idea for kids today. "Actually, it was dumb," he says.

KEN GREENE
6-2, 198
ST. LOUIS CARDINALS

The Cardinals had two first-round draft choices last year. First, they went for Steve Little, a great punter and place-kicker. Then they snatched Ken Greene away from an army of pickers who wanted a potentially great defensive back.... Greene was more than potential. An All-America at Washington State, he was touted as an athlete who was never satisfied to give just 100% of his effort. He always had to dig up a bit more.... So, the first thing the Cardinal coaches noted was his intensity.... And then there was his ball-hawking against the pass and his vicious contact on runners. One of the things that helped him was the fact that he'd been a star receiver in high school and had a good idea of pass routes.... It all added up to a rookie starting in the NFL.

Safety
JOHN HARRIS
6-2, 200
SEATTLE SEAHAWKS

All the NFL teams kept passing up on John Harris in the annual draft. Finally, the Seahawks decided to take him on the seventh round. They were lucky they did — and 27 other clubs now wish they hadn't been so picky.... Harris, from Arizona State, was big, fast, and tough, but it takes a lot of brains to play secondary defense in the NFL.... Great quarterbacks can pick apart the zone defenses.... Receivers run such slick pass patterns.... Defending against them takes a lot of savvy.... Well, everyone should have known Harris was smart. He was number one in his class in high school and for three years he made the All-Academic team in the Western Athletic Conference.... And from the first day in pro camp he proved he was fast enough and tough enough. The rest of the NFL discovered it soon enough.

1978 FINAL STANDINGS AMERICAN FOOTBALL CONFERENCE

EASTERN DIVISION

	W	L	T	Pct.	Pts.	OP
* New England	11	5	0	.688	358	286
# Miami	11	5	0	.688	372	254
N.Y. Jets	8	8	0	.500	359	364
Buffalo	5	11	0	.313	302	354
Baltimore	5	11	0	.313	239	421

CENTRAL DIVISION

	W	L	T	Pct.	Pts.	OP
* Pittsburgh	14	2	0	.875	356	195
# Houston	10	6	0	.625	283	298
Cleveland	8	8	0	.500	334	356
Cincinnati	4	12	0	.250	252	284

WESTERN DIVISION

	W	L	T	Pct.	Pts.	OP
* Denver	10	6	0	.625	282	198
Oakland	9	7	0	.563	311	283
Seattle	9	7	0	.563	345	358
San Diego	9	7	0	.563	355	309
Kansas City	4	12	0	.250	243	327

*Division Champion
#Wild Card for Playoffs

AFC Playoffs
AFC First Round
Houston 17, Miami 9
Playoffs
Pittsburgh 33, Denver 10
Houston 31, New England 14
AFC Championship
Pittsburgh 34, Houston 5
Super Bowl XIII
Pittsburgh 35, Dallas 31

...And Previews for 1979 $\longrightarrow$

EASTERN DIVISION

Baltimore Colts

Bert Jones...With his injury healed, this star QB should put Colts into Super Bowl picture.

QUARTERBACKING:
RUNNING:
RECEIVING:
OFFENSIVE LINE:
DEFENSE:

Miami Dolphins

Delvin Williams...The surprise rusher of last year is headed for even better things.

QUARTERBACKING:
RUNNING:
RECEIVING:
OFFENSIVE LINE:
DEFENSE:

New England Patriots

Russ Francis...The big tight end does it all as receiver and a crunching blocker.

QUARTERBACKING:
RUNNING:
RECEIVING:
OFFENSIVE LINE:
DEFENSE:

New York Jets

Greg Buttle...Hard-nosed linebacker is the club's key man against the running game.

QUARTERBACKING:
RUNNING:
RECEIVING:
OFFENSIVE LINE:
DEFENSE:

Buffalo Bills

Reggie McKenzie...With Joe DeLamielleure, he gives Bills best brace of guards in NFL.

QUARTERBACKING:	🏈 🏈 🏈
RUNNING:	🏈 🏈 🏈◖
RECEIVING:	🏈 🏈 🏈◖
OFFENSIVE LINE:	🏈 🏈 🏈◖
DEFENSE:	🏈 🏈 🏈

WESTERN DIVISION

Denver Broncos

Rob Lytle...This may be the year for this tough runner to reach stardom.

QUARTERBACKING:	🏈 🏈 🏈
RUNNING:	🏈 🏈 🏈 🏈
RECEIVING:	🏈 🏈 🏈 🏈
OFFENSIVE LINE:	🏈 🏈 🏈 🏈◖
DEFENSE:	🏈 🏈 🏈 🏈 🏈◖

San Diego Chargers

Dan Fouts...With a better supporting cast, he'd be one of the NFL's best QBs.

QUARTERBACKING:
RUNNING:
RECEIVING:
OFFENSIVE LINE:
DEFENSE:

Oakland Raiders

Mark van Eeghen...The power runner in the Raider offense gets the tough yardage.

QUARTERBACKING:
RUNNING:
RECEIVING:
OFFENSIVE LINE:
DEFENSE:

Seattle Seahawks

Jim Zorn...No longer the "underrated QB," he's now a star in his own right.

QUARTERBACKING:	
RUNNING:	
RECEIVING:	
OFFENSIVE LINE:	
DEFENSE:	

Kansas City Chiefs

Gary Spani...This rising young linebacking star is one of Chiefs' key defenders.

QUARTERBACKING:	
RUNNING:	
RECEIVING:	
OFFENSIVE LINE:	
DEFENSE:	

CENTRAL DIVISION

Pittsburgh Steelers

Franco Harris...His power rushing helps make Steelers Super Bowl choice again.

QUARTERBACKING:
RUNNING:
RECEIVING:
OFFENSIVE LINE:
DEFENSE:

Houston Oilers

Dan Pastorini...Slick QB's passing provides alternate threat to Campbell's running.

QUARTERBACKING:
RUNNING:
RECEIVING:
OFFENSIVE LINE:
DEFENSE:

Cincinnati Bengals

Pete Johnson...The big full-back has explosive power and is a fine pass receiver.

QUARTERBACKING:
RUNNING:
RECEIVING:
OFFENSIVE LINE:
DEFENSE:

Cleveland Browns

Brian Sipe...The Browns' improvement last year should continue under his quarterbacking.

QUARTERBACKING:
RUNNING:
RECEIVING:
OFFENSIVE LINE:
DEFENSE:

1978 FINAL STANDINGS
NATIONAL FOOTBALL
CONFERENCE

EASTERN DIVISION

	W	L	T	Pct.	Pts.	OP
* Dallas	12	4	0	.750	384	208
# Philadelphia	9	7	0	.563	270	250
Washington	8	8	0	.500	273	283
St. Louis	6	10	0	.375	248	296
N.Y. Giants	6	10	0	.375	264	298

CENTRAL DIVISION

	W	L	T	Pct.	Pts.	OP
* Minnesota	8	7	1	.531	294	306
Green Bay	8	7	1	.531	249	269
Detroit	7	9	0	.438	290	300
Chicago	7	9	0	.438	253	274
Tampa Bay	5	11	0	.313	241	259

WESTERN DIVISION

	W	L	T	Pct.	Pts.	OP
* Los Angeles	12	4	0	.750	316	245
# Atlanta	9	7	0	.563	240	290
New Orleans	7	9	0	.438	281	298
San Francisco	2	14	0	.125	219	350

*Division Champion
#Wild Card for Playoffs

NFC Playoffs
NFC First Round
Atlanta 14, Philadelphia 13
PLAYOFFS
Dallas 27, Atlanta 20
Los Angeles 34, Minnesota 10
NFC Championship
Dallas 28, Los Angeles 0
Super Bowl XIII
Pittsburgh 35, Dallas 31

...And Previews for 1979 $\longrightarrow$

EASTERN DIVISION

Dallas Cowboys

Tony Dorsett...Another year and he'll come into NFL superstar status as a runner.

QUARTERBACKING:
RUNNING:
RECEIVING:
OFFENSIVE LINE:
DEFENSE:

Philadelphia Eagles

Bill Bergey...One of the NFL's best linebackers who just missed All-Pro.

QUARTERBACKING:
RUNNING:
RECEIVING:
OFFENSIVE LINE:
DEFENSE:

New York Giants

Harry Carson...A lot of experts say he's as good a linebacker as anyone has.

QUARTERBACKING: 🏈 🏈 ◖
RUNNING: 🏈 🏈
RECEIVING: 🏈 🏈 🏈
OFFENSIVE LINE: 🏈 🏈 🏈
DEFENSE: 🏈 🏈 🏈

St. Louis Cardinals

Mel Gray...The little speedster is easily one of the best wide receivers in football.

QUARTERBACKING: 🏈 🏈 🏈 ◖
RUNNING: 🏈 🏈 🏈
RECEIVING: 🏈 🏈 🏈 ◖
OFFENSIVE LINE: 🏈 🏈 🏈 🏈
DEFENSE: 🏈 🏈 ◖

Washington Redskins

Ken Houston...At age 34, he continues to pull off the great plays as a safety.

QUARTERBACKING:
RUNNING:
RECEIVING:
OFFENSIVE LINE:
DEFENSE:

WESTERN DIVISION

Los Angeles Rams

Larry Brooks...Tough defensive tackle is the inside anchor of Rams' front four.

QUARTERBACKING:
RUNNING:
RECEIVING:
OFFENSIVE LINE:
DEFENSE:

San Francisco 49ers

O.J. Simpson...The Juice would like his final season to be one to remember.

QUARTERBACKING:
RUNNING:
RECEIVING:
OFFENSIVE LINE:
DEFENSE:

Atlanta Falcons

Steve Bartkowski...Falcons are flying higher on this QB's strong right arm.

QUARTERBACKING:
RUNNING:
RECEIVING:
OFFENSIVE LINE:
DEFENSE:

New Orleans Saints

Archie Mannie... He was the comeback QB of 1978, but the Saints need much more.

QUARTERBACKING:
RUNNING:
RECEIVING:
OFFENSIVE LINE:
DEFENSE:

CENTRAL DIVISION

Minnesota Vikings

Matt Blair... Veteran linebacker is the glue for the Vikes' defense up front.

QUARTERBACKING:
RUNNING:
RECEIVING:
OFFENSIVE LINE:
DEFENSE:

Chicago Bears

Dennis Lick...Hard-nosed tackle helps clear the way for Walter Payton's ground gaining.

QUARTERBACKING:

RUNNING:

RECEIVING:

OFFENSIVE LINE:

DEFENSE:

Green Bay Packers

Mark Koncar...The Pack counts on him to lead offensive charge from tackle position.

QUARTERBACKING:

RUNNING:

RECEIVING:

OFFENSIVE LINE:

DEFENSE:

Tampa Bay Buccaneers

Ricky Bell...A tough, slashing runner who makes the Bucs' ground game go.

QUARTERBACKING:
RUNNING:
RECEIVING:
OFFENSIVE LINE:
DEFENSE:

Detroit Lions

Gary Danielson...The Lions' attack depends mostly on his cool, sharp passing.

QUARTERBACKING:
RUNNING:
RECEIVING:
OFFENSIVE LINE:
DEFENSE:

HOW THEY'RE PICKED TO FINISH IN 1979

AFC

East	West	Central
1. Baltimore 5	1. Denver 2	1. Pittsburgh 2
2. Miami 1	2. San Diego 1	2. Houston 1
3. New England 2	3. Oakland 3	3. Cincinnati 4
4. New York Jets 3	4. Seattle 4	4. Cleveland 3
5. Buffalo 4	5. Kansas City 5	

NFC

East	West	Central
1. Dallas 2	1. Los Angeles 5	1. Minnesota 3
2. Philadelphia 1	2. San Francisco 4	2. Chicago 2
3. New York Giants 4	3. Atlanta 2	3. Green Bay 4
4. St. Louis 5	4. New Orleans 1	4. Tampa Bay 1
5. Washington 3		5. Detroit 5

Super Bowl XIV
Pittsburgh vs. Dallas

NFC West phil. Houston

Best Bet for
Rookie-of-the-Year
Sorry! It's up for grabs in '79!

1978 RECORDS

SCORING

INDIVIDUAL CHAMPION
NFC: 118 Frank Corral, Los Angeles (Kicker)
AFC: 107 Pat Leahy, New York Jets (Kicker)
Touchdowns
AFC: 90 David Sims, Seattle
NFC: 72 Terdell Middleton, Green Bay

TOUCHDOWNS
AFC: 15 David Sims, Seattle (14 Rushing; 1 Reception)
NFC: 12 Terdell Middleton, Green Bay (11 Rushing; 1
Reception)

EXTRA POINTS
NFC: 46 Rafael Septien, Dallas (47 Attempts)
AFC: 44 Roy Gerela, Pittsburgh (45 Attempts)

FIELD GOALS
NFC: 29 Frank Corral, Los Angeles (43 Attempts)
AFC: 22 Pat Leahy, New York Jets (30 Attempts)

ONE GAME PERFORMANCE
AFC: 24 (4 TDs) Earl Campbell, Houston vs Miami,
November 20
NFC: 24 (4 TDs) Terdell Middleton, Green Bay vs Seattle,
October 15; Wilbert Montgomery, Philadelphia vs Washington,
September 10

TEAM LEADERS
AFC: BALTIMORE 51 Toni Linhart; BUFFALO 66 Tom Dempsey;
CINCINNATI 74 Chris Bahr; CLEVELAND 94 Don Cockroft;

DENVER 64 Jim Turner; HOUSTON 78 Earl Campbell; KANSAS
CITY 85 Jan Stenerud; MIAMI 98 Garo Yepremian; NEW
ENGLAND 66 Horace Ivory; NEW YORK JETS 107 Pat Leahy;
OAKLAND 69 Errol Mann; PITTSBURGH 80 Roy Gerela; SAN
DIEGO 91 Rolf Benirschke; SEATTLE 90 David Sims

NFC: ATLANTA 57 Tim Mazzetti; CHICAGO 77 Bob Thomas;
DALLAS 94 Rafael Septien; DETROIT 92 Benny Ricardo;
GREEN BAY 72 Terdell Middleton; LOS ANGELES 118 Frank
Corral; MINNESOTA 72 Rick Danmeier; NEW ORLEANS 42
Tony Galbreath & Chuck Muncie; NEW YORK GIANTS 90 Joe
Danelo; PHILADELPHIA 60 Wilbert Montgomery; ST. LOUIS
60 Jim Bakken; SAN FRANCISCO 69 Ray Wersching; TAMPA
BAY 64 Neil O'Donoghue; WASHINGTON 87 Mark Moseley

TEAM CHAMPION

NFC:	384	Dallas
AFC:	372	Miami

TOP TEN SCORERS — TOUCHDOWNS

	TDs Tot	TDs Rush	TDs Pass	TDs Misc	Tot Pts
Sims, David, Sea.	15	14	1	0	90
Campbell, Earl, Hou.	13	13	0	0	78
Jefferson, John, S.D.	13	0	13	0	78
Middleton, Terdell, G.B.	12	11	1	0	72
Ivory, Horace, N.E.	11	11	0	0	66
Payton, Walter, Chi.	11	11	0	0	66
Swann, Lynn, Pitt.	11	0	11	0	66
Casper, Dave, Oak.	10	0	9	1	60
Dorsett, Tony, Dall.	10	7	2	1	60
Long, Kevin, N.Y.J.	10	10	0	0	60

TOP TEN SCORERS — KICKING

	XP Made	XP Att	FG Made	FG Att	Tot Pts
Corral, Frank, L.A.	31	33	29	43	118
Leahy, Pat, N.Y.J.	41	42	22	30	107

Yepremian, Garo, Mia.	41	45	19	23	98
Cockroft, Don, Clev.	37	40	19	28	94
Septien, Rafael, Dall.	46	47	16	26	94
Ricardo, Benny, Det.	32	33	20	28	92
Benirschke, Rolf, S.D.	37	43	18	22	91
Danelo, Joe, N.Y.G.	27	29	21	29	90
Moseley, Mark, Wash.	30	31	19	30	87
Stenerud, Jan, K.C.	25	26	20	30	85

AFC — INDIVIDUALS

	TD	R	P	M	XP	XPA	FG	FGA	PTS
Leahy, Pat, N.Y.J.	0	0	0	0	41	42	22	30	107
Yepremian, Garo, Mia. .	0	0	0	0	41	45	19	23	98
Cockroft, Don, Clev. ..	0	0	0	0	37	40	19	28	94
Benirschke, Rolf, S.D. .	0	0	0	0	37	43	18	22	91
Sims, David, Sea.	15	14	1	0	0	0	0	0	90
Stenerud, Jan, K.C. ...	0	0	0	0	25	26	20	30	85
Gerela, Roy, Pitt.	0	0	0	0	44	45	12	26	80
Herrera, Efren, Sea.	0	0	0	0	40	44	13	21	79
Campbell, Earl, Hou. ..	13	13	0	0	0	0	0	0	78
Jefferson, John, S.D. .	13	0	13	0	0	0	0	0	78

NFC — INDIVIDUALS

	TD	R	P	M	XP	XPA	FG	FGA	PTS
Corral, Frank, L.A.	0	0	0	0	31	33	29	43	118
Septien, Rafael, Dall. ..	0	0	0	0	46	47	16	26	94
Ricardo, Benny, Det. ..	0	0	0	0	32	33	20	28	92
Danelo, Joe, N.Y.G. ...	0	0	0	0	27	29	21	29	90
Moseley, Mark, Wash. .	0	0	0	0	30	31	19	30	87
Thomas, Bob, Chi.	0	0	0	0	26	28	17	22	77
Danmeier, Rick, Minn. .	0	0	0	0	36	37	12	19	72
Middleton, Terdell, G.B.	12	11	1	0	0	0	0	0	72
Wersching, Ray, S.F. ..	0	0	0	0	24	25	15	23	69
Payton, Walter, Chi.	11	11	0	0	0	0	0	0	66

RUSHING

INDIVIDUAL CHAMPION
AFC: 1450 (Yards)   Earl Campbell, Houston
NFC: 1395 (Yards)   Walter Payton, Chicago

AVERAGE
AFC: 6.0 (Yards)   Ted McKnight, Kansas City (627 Yards; 104 Attempts)
NFC: 4.7 (Yards)   Wilbert Montgomery, Philadelphia (1220 Yards; 259 Attempts)

TOUCHDOWNS
AFC: 14   David Sims, Seattle
NFC: 11   Terdell Middleton, Green Bay; Walter Payton, Chicago

ATTEMPTS
NFC: 333   Walter Payton, Chicago
AFC: 310   Franco Harris, Pittsburgh

LONGEST
AFC: 81 (Yards)   Earl Campbell, Houston vs Miami, November 20 (TD)
NFC: 76 (Yards)   Terdell Middleton, Green Bay vs Detroit, October 1 (TD); Walter Payton, Chicago vs Denver, October 16

ONE GAME PERFORMANCE
AFC: 208 (Yards; 21 Attempts)   Terry Miller, Buffalo vs New York Giants, November 26
NFC: 157 (Yards; 22 Attempts)   Walter Payton, Chicago vs Denver, October 16

TEAM LEADERS
AFC: BALTIMORE 956 Joe Washington; BUFFALO 1060 Terry Miller; CINCINNATI 762 Pete Johnson; CLEVELAND 960 Greg Pruitt; DENVER 455 Lonnie Perrin; HOUSTON 1450 Earl Campbell; KANSAS CITY 1053 Tony Reed; MIAMI 1258 Delvin Williams; NEW ENGLAND 768 Sam Cunningham; NEW YORK

JETS 954 Kevin Long; OAKLAND 1080 Mark van Eeghen;
PITTSBURGH 1082 Franco Harris; SAN DIEGO 820 Lydell
Mitchell; SEATTLE 805 Sherman Smith

NFC: ATLANTA 707 Bubba Bean; CHICAGO 1395 Walter Payton;
DALLAS 1325 Tony Dorsett; DETROIT 924 Dexter Bussey; GREEN
BAY 1116 Terdell Middleton; LOS ANGELES 658 Cullen Bryant;
MINNESOTA 749 Chuck Foreman; NEW ORLEANS 635 Tony
Galbreath; NEW YORK GIANTS 625 Doug Kotar; PHILADELPHIA
1220 Wilbert Montgomery; ST. LOUIS 664 Jim Otis; SAN
FRANCISCO 593 O.J. Simpson; TAMPA BAY 679 Ricky Bell;
WASHINGTON 1014 John Riggins

TEAM CHAMPION

AFC: 3165 (Yards) New England
NFC: 2783 (Yards) Dallas

TOP TEN RUSHERS

	Att	Yards	Avg	Long	TD
Campbell, Earl, Hou.	302	1450	4.8	t81	13
Payton, Walter, Chi.	333	1395	4.2	76	11
Dorsett, Tony, Dall.	290	1325	4.6	63	7
Williams, Delvin, Mia.	272	1258	4.6	58	8
Montgomery, Wilbert, Phil. . .	259	1220	4.7	47	9
Middleton, Terdell, G.B.	284	1116	3.9	t76	11
Harris, Franco, Pitt.	310	1082	3.5	37	8
van Eeghen, Mark, Oak.	270	1080	4.0	34	9
Miller, Terry, Buff.	238	1060	4.5	t60	7
Reed, Tony, K.C.	206	1053	5.1	t62	5

AFC — INDIVIDUALS

	Att	Yards	Avg	Long	TD
Campbell, Earl, Hou.	302	1450	4.8	t81	13
Williams, Delvin, Mia.	272	1258	4.6	58	8
Harris, Franco, Pitt.	310	1082	3.5	37	8
van Eeghen, Mark, Oak.	270	1080	4.0	34	9
Miller, Terry, Buff.	238	1060	4.5	t60	7

Reed, Tony, K.C.	206	1053	5.1	t62	5
Pruitt, Greg, Clev.	176	960	5.5	t70	3
Washington, Joe, Balt.	240	956	4.0	29	0
Long, Kevin, N.Y.J.	214	954	4.5	27	10
Mitchell, Lydell, S.D.	214	820	3.8	25	3
Smith, Sherman, Sea.	165	805	4.9	67	6
Cunningham, Sam, N.E.	199	768	3.9	t52	8
Johnson, Pete, Cin.	180	762	4.2	t50	7
Sims, David, Sea.	174	752	4.3	t44	14
Ivory, Horace, N.E.	141	693	4.9	28	11

NFC — INDIVIDUALS

	Att	Yards	Avg	Long	TD
Payton, Walter, Chi.	333	1395	4.2	76	11
Dorsett, Tony, Dall.	290	1325	4.6	63	7
Montgomery, Wilbert, Phil. ..	259	1220	4.7	47	9
Middleton, Terdell, G.B.	284	1116	3.9	t76	11
Riggins, John, Wash.	248	1014	4.1	31	5
Harper, Roland, Chi.	240	992	4.1	31	6
Bussey, Dexter, Det.	225	924	4.1	36	5
Foreman, Chuck, Minn.	237	749	3.2	21	5
Bean, Bubba, Atl.	193	707	3.7	t25	3
Bell, Ricky, T.B.	185	679	3.7	56	6
Otis, Jim, St.L.	197	664	3.4	17	8
King, Horace, Det.	155	660	4.3	t75	4
Bryant, Cullen, L.A.	178	658	3.7	26	7
Galbreath, Tony, N.O.	186	635	3.4	t20	5
Morris, Wayne, St.L.	174	631	3.6	27	1

PASSING

INDIVIDUAL CHAMPION
NFC: 84.9 (Rating Points) Roger Staubach, Dallas
AFC: 84.8 (Rating Points) Terry Bradshaw, Pittsburgh

ATTEMPTS
NFC: 572 Fran Tarkenton, Minnesota
AFC: 443 Jim Zorn, Seattle

COMPLETIONS
NFC: 345 Fran Tarkenton, Minnesota
AFC: 248 Jim Zorn, Seattle

COMPLETION PERCENTAGE
AFC: 63.0 Bob Griese, Miami (235 Attempts; 148 Completions)
NFC: 61.8 Archie Manning, New Orleans (471 Attempts; 291 Completions)

YARDAGE
NFC: 3468 Fran Tarkenton, Minnesota
AFC: 3283 Jim Zorn, Seattle

TOUCHDOWN PASSES
AFC: 28 Terry Bradshaw, Pittsburgh
NFC: 25 Roger Staubach, Dallas;
~~Fran Tarkenton, Minnesota~~

MOST INTERCEPTIONS
NFC: 32 Fran Tarkenton, Minnesota (572 Attempts)
AFC: 30 Ken Stabler, Oakland (406 Attempts)

LOWEST PERCENTAGE, PASSES HAD INTERCEPTED
AFC: 3.0 Craig Morton, Denver (267 Attempts; 8 Intercepted)
NFC: 3.4 Archie Manning, New Orleans (471 Attempts; 16 Intercepted)

TEAM CHAMPION
NFC: 83.1 (Rating Points) Dallas
AFC: 82.9 (Rating Points) Miami

TOP TEN INDIVIDUAL QUALIFIERS

	Att	Comp	Pct Comp	Yards	Int	Rating Points
Staubach, Roger, Dall.	413	231	55.9	3190	16	84.9
Bradshaw, Terry, Pitt.	368	207	56.3	2915	20	84.8
Fouts, Dan, S.D.	381	224	58.8	2999	20	83.2
Griese, Bob, Mia.	235	148	63.0	1791	11	82.4
Manning, Archie, N.O.	471	291	61.8	3416	16	81.6
Sipe, Brian, Clev.	399	222	55.6	2906	15	80.6
Morton, Craig, Den.	267	146	54.7	1802	8	77.0
Danielson, Gary, Det.	351	199	56.7	2294	17	73.6
Zorn, Jim, Sea.	443	248	56.0	3283	20	72.2
Ferguson, Joe, Buff.	330	175	53.0	2136	15	70.5

AFC INDIVIDUAL QUALIFIERS

	Att	Comp	Pct Comp	Yards	Int	Rating Points
Bradshaw, Terry, Pitt.	368	207	56.3	2915	20	84.8
Fouts, Dan, S.D.	381	224	58.8	2999	20	83.2
Griese, Bob, Mia.	235	148	63.0	1791	11	82.4
Sipe, Brian, Clev.	399	222	55.6	2906	15	80.6
Morton, Craig, Den.	267	146	54.7	1802	8	77.0
Zorn, Jim, Sea.	443	248	56.0	3283	20	72.2
Ferguson, Joe, Buff.	330	175	53.0	2136	15	70.5
Pastorini, Dan, Hou.	368	199	54.1	2473	17	70.3
Robinson, Matt, N.Y.J.	266	124	46.6	2002	16	63.6
Grogan, Steve, N.E.	362	181	50.0	2824	23	63.3
Stabler, Ken, Oak.	406	237	58.4	2944	30	63.1
Anderson, Ken, Cin.	319	173	54.2	2219	22	57.8
Livingston, Mike, K.C.	290	159	54.8	1573	13	57.3
Troup, Bill, Balt.	296	154	52.0	1882	21	53.7

NFC INDIVIDUAL QUALIFIERS

	Att	Comp	Pct Comp	Yards	Int	Rating Points
Staubach, Roger, Dall.	413	231	55.9	3190	16	84.9
Manning, Archie, N.O.	471	291	61.8	3416	16	81.6
Danielson, Gary, Det.	351	199	56.7	2294	17	73.6
Tarkenton, Fran, Minn.	572	345	60.3	3468	32	68.9

Jaworski, Ron, Phil.	398	206	51.8	2487	16	68.0
Hart, Jim, St.L.	477	240	50.3	3121	18	66.8
Haden, Pat, L.A.	444	229	51.6	2995	19	65.0
Theismann, Joe, Wash.	390	187	47.9	2593	18	61.6
Bartkowski, Steve, Atl.	369	187	50.7	2489	18	61.1
Whitehurst, David, G.B.	328	168	51.2	2093	17	59.7
Avellini, Bob, Chi.	264	141	53.4	1718	16	54.6
Williams, Doug, T.B.	194	73	37.6	1170	8	53.5
Pisarcik, Joe, N.Y.G.	301	143	47.5	2096	23	52.3
DeBerg, Steve, S.F.	302	137	45.4	1570	22	39.8

PASS RECEIVING

INDIVIDUAL CHAMPION
NFC: 88 Rickey Young, Minnesota
AFC: 71 Steve Largent, Seattle

YARDAGE
AFC: 1169 Wesley Walker, New York Jets
NFC: 1072 Harold Carmichael, Philadelphia

AVERAGE GAIN
AFC: 24.4 Wesley Walker, New York Jets (48 Receptions; 1169 Yards)
NFC: 20.0 Morris Owens, Tampa Bay (32 Receptions; 640 Yards)

TOUCHDOWNS
AFC: 13 John Jefferson, San Diego
NFC: 9 Billy Joe Dupree, Dallas; Sammy White, Minnesota

LONGEST
AFC: 92 (Yards) Frank Lewis, Buffalo vs Miami, September 17 (from Joe Ferguson, TD)
NFC: 91 (Yards) Tony Dorsett, Dallas vs Baltimore, September 4 (from Roger Staubach, TD)

ONE GAME PERFORMANCE

NFC: 14 (122 Yards)   Tony Galbreath, New Orleans vs Green Bay, September 10

AFC: 10 (88 Yards)   Don McCauley, Baltimore vs Seattle, November 12

TEAM LEADERS

AFC: BALTIMORE 45 Joe Washington; BUFFALO 44 Bob Chandler; CINCINNATI 47 Isaac Curtis; CLEVELAND 43 Reggie Rucker; DENVER 54 Riley Odoms; HOUSTON 47 Ken Burrough; KANSAS CITY 48 Tony Reed; MIAMI 48 Nat Moore; NEW ENGLAND 39 Russ Francis; NEW YORK JETS 48 Wesley Walker; OAKLAND 62 Dave Casper; PITTSBURGH 61 Lynn Swann; SAN DIEGO 57 Lydell Mitchell; SEATTLE 71 Steve Largent

NFC: ATLANTA 45 Wallace Francis & Billy Ryckman; CHICAGO 50 Walter Payton; DALLAS 47 Preston Pearson; DETROIT 53 David Hill; GREEN BAY 46 James Lofton; LOS ANGELES 50 Willie Miller; MINNESOTA 88 Rickey Young; NEW ORLEANS 74 Tony Galbreath; NEW YORK GIANTS 32 Johnny Perkins & Jimmy Robinson; PHILADELPHIA 55 Harold Carmichael; ST. LOUIS 62 Pat Tilley; SAN FRANCISCO 31 Freddie Solomon; TAMPA BAY 32 Morris Owens; WASHINGTON 36 Danny Buggs

TOP TEN PASS RECEIVERS

	No	Yards	Avg	Long	TD
Young, Rickey, Minn.	88	704	8.0	48	5
Galbreath, Tony, N.O.	74	582	7.9	35	2
Largent, Steve, Sea.	71	1168	16.5	t57	8
Rashad, Ahmad, Minn.	66	769	11.7	t58	8
Tilley, Pat, St.L.	62	900	14.5	43	3
Casper, Dave, Oak.	62	852	13.7	44	9
Swann, Lynn, Pitt.	61	880	14.4	62	11
Foreman, Chuck, Minn.	61	396	6.5	20	2
Mitchell, Lydell, S.D.	57	500	8.8	t55	2
Jefferson, John, S.D.	56	1001	17.9	t46	13

AFC — INDIVIDUALS

	No	Yards	Avg	Long	TD
Largent, Steve, Sea.	71	1168	16.5	t57	8
Casper, Dave, Oak.	62	852	13.7	44	9
Swann, Lynn, Pitt.	61	880	14.4	62	11
Mitchell, Lydell, S.D.	57	500	8.8	t55	2
Jefferson, John, S.D.	56	1001	17.9	t46	13
Odoms, Riley, Den.	54	829	15.4	t42	6
Branch, Cliff, Oak.	49	709	14.5	41	1
Walker, Wesley, N.Y.J.	48	1169	24.4	t77	8
Moore, Nat, Mia.	48	645	13.4	47	10
Reed, Tony, K.C.	48	483	10.1	44	1
Curtis, Isaac, Cin.	47	737	15.7	57	3
Burrough, Ken, Hou.	47	624	13.3	44	2
Harris, Duriel, Mia.	45	654	14.5	t63	3
Washington, Joe, Balt.	45	377	8.4	33	1
Chandler, Bob, Buff.	44	581	13.2	44	5

NFC — INDIVIDUALS

	No	Yards	Avg	Long	TD
Young, Rickey, Minn.	88	704	8.0	48	5
Galbreath, Tony, N.O.	74	582	7.9	35	2
Rashad, Ahmad, Minn.	66	769	11.7	t58	8
Tilley, Pat, St.L.	62	900	14.5	43	3
Foreman, Chuck, Minn.	61	396	6.5	20	2
Carmichael, Harold, Phil.	55	1072	19.5	t56	8
Childs, Henry, N.O.	53	869	16.4	52	4
White, Sammy, Minn.	53	741	14.0	t33	9
Hill, David, Det.	53	633	11.9	32	4
Miller, Willie, L.A.	50	767	15.3	52	5
Payton, Walter, Chi.	50	480	9.6	61	0
Jessie, Ron, L.A.	49	752	15.3	49	4
King, Horace, Det.	48	396	8.3	34	2
Tucker, Bob, Minn.	47	540	11.5	35	0
Pearson, Preston, Dall.	47	526	11.2	34	0

INTERCEPTIONS

INDIVIDUAL CHAMPION
AFC: 10 Thom Darden, Cleveland
NFC: 9 - Willie Buchanon, Green Bay;
       Ken Stone, St. Louis

YARDAGE
AFC: 200 Thom Darden, Cleveland
NFC: 167 Tom Myers, New Orleans

TOUCHDOWNS
NFC: 3 Rod Perry, Los Angeles
AFC: 2 Lyle Blackwood, Baltimore; Scott Perry, Cincinnati

LONGEST
NFC: 97 (Yards) Tom Myers, New Orleans vs Minnesota,
       September 3 (TD)
AFC: 85 (Yards) Charles Romes, Buffalo vs New York Jets,
       September 10 (TD)

TEAM LEADERS
AFC: BALTIMORE 6 Norm Thompson; BUFFALO 5 Mario Clark;
      CINCINNATI 4 Dick Jauron; CLEVELAND 10 Thom Darden;
      DENVER 6 Steve Foley & Bernard Jackson; HOUSTON 5 Willie
      Alexander; KANSAS CITY 6 Tim Gray; MIAMI 6 Tim Foley;
      NEW ENGLAND 6 Mike Haynes; NEW YORK JETS 5 Bobby
      Jackson & Burgess Owens; OAKLAND 6 Charles Phillips;
      PITTSBURGH 6 Tony Dungy; SAN DIEGO 4 Mike Fuller;
      SEATTLE 5 Cornell Webster
NFC: ATLANTA 6 Rolland Lawrence; CHICAGO 4 Gary Fencik;
      DALLAS 5 Benny Barnes; DETROIT 5 Jim Allen; GREEN BAY 9
      Willie Buchanon; LOS ANGELES 8 Rod Perry & Pat Thomas;
      MINNESOTA 7 Bobby Bryant; NEW ORLEANS 6 Tom Myers;
      NEW YORK GIANTS 7 Terry Jackson; PHILADELPHIA 7
      Herman Edwards; ST. LOUIS 9 Ken Stone; SAN FRANCISCO 6
      Chuck Crist; TAMPA BAY 6 Cedric Brown; WASHINGTON 7
      Jake Scott

TEAM CHAMPION

AFC: 32 Miami
NFC: 29 Tampa Bay

TOP TEN INTERCEPTORS

	No	Yards	Avg	Long	TD
Darden, Thom, Clev.	10	200	20.0	46	0
Stone, Ken, St.L.	9	139	15.4	33	0
Buchanon, Willie, G.B.	9	93	10.3	t77	1
Perry, Rod, L.A.	8	117	14.6	t44	3
Thomas, Pat, L.A.	8	96	12.0	t33	1
Jackson, Terry, N.Y.G.	7	115	16.4	51	1
Scott, Jake, Wash.	7	72	10.3	39	0
Bryant, Bobby, Minn.	7	69	9.9	23	0
Edwards, Herman, Phil.	7	59	8.4	25	0
14 tied with	6				

AFC — INDIVIDUALS

	No	Yards	Avg	Long	TD
Darden, Thom, Clev.	10	200	20.0	46	0
Jackson, Bernard, Den.	6	128	21.3	38	0
Haynes, Mike, N.E.	6	123	20.5	50	1
Phillips, Charles, Oak.	6	121	20.2	t42	1
Gray, Tim, K.C.	6	118	19.7	61	0
Dungy, Tony, Pitt.	6	95	15.8	65	0
Foley, Steve, Den.	6	84	14.0	30	0
Davis, Oliver, Clev.	6	65	10.8	33	1
Thompson, Norm, Balt.	6	52	8.7	31	0
Foley, Tim, Mia.	6	12	2.0	8	0
Owens, Burgess, N.Y.J.	5	156	31.2	49	1
Nelson, Steve, N.E.	5	104	20.8	37	0
Alexander, Willie, Hou.	5	51	10.2	29	0
Clark, Mario, Buff.	5	29	5.8	29	0
Jackson, Bobby, N.Y.J.	5	26	5.2	13	0
Webster, Cornell, Sea.	5	9	1.8	14	0

t = Touchdown

NFC — INDIVIDUALS

	No	Yards	Avg	Long	TD
Stone, Ken, St.L.	9	139	15.4	33	0
Buchanon, Willie, G.B.	9	93	10.3	t77	1
Perry, Rod, L.A.	8	117	14.6	t44	3
Thomas, Pat, L.A.	8	96	12.0	t33	1
Jackson, Terry, N.Y.G.	7	115	16.4	51	1
Scott, Jake, Wash.	7	72	10.3	39	0
Bryant, Bobby, Minn.	7	69	9.9	23	0
Edwards, Herman, Phil.	7	59	8.4	25	0
Myers, Tom, N.O.	6	167	27.8	t97	1
Crist, Chuck, S.F.	6	159	26.5	32	0
Brown, Cedric, T.B.	6	110	18.3	29	0
Lawrence, Rolland, Atl.	6	76	12.7	44	0
Allen, Carl, St.L.	6	54	9.0	21	0

PUNTING

INDIVIDUAL CHAMPION

AFC: 43.1 (Yard Average) Pat McInally, Cincinnati (91 Punts; 3919 Yards)

NFC: 42.5 (Yard Average) Tom Skladany, Detroit (86 Punts; 3654 Yards)

NET AVERAGE

AFC: 35.2 (Yard Average) Craig Colquitt, Pittsburgh (66 Total Punts; 2323 Net Yards)

NFC: 35.0 (Yard Average) Tom Skladany, Detroit (87 Total Punts; 3047 Net Yards)

LONGEST

NFC: 81 (Yards) Mike Wood, St. Louis vs New York Giants, December 10

AFC: 79 (Yards) Chuck Ramsey, New York Jets vs Baltimore, October 15

MOST

NFC: 109 John James, Atlanta

AFC: 96 Bucky Dilts, Denver

TEAM CHAMPION

AFC: 42.4 (Yard Average) Cincinnati

NFC: 42.1 (Yard Average) New York Giants

TOP TEN PUNTERS

	Punts	Yards	Long	Avg
McInally, Pat, Cin.	91	3919	65	43.1
Guy, Ray, Oak.	81	3462	69	42.7
Skladany, Tom, Det.	86	3654	63	42.5
Jennings, Dave, N.Y.G.	95	3995	68	42.1
Blanchard, Tom, N.O.	84	3532	61	42.0
Andrusyshyn, Zenon, K.C.	79	3247	61	41.1
Green, Dave, T.B.	100	4092	61	40.9
White, Danny, Dall.	76	3076	56	40.5
Roberts, George, Mia.	81	3263	59	40.3
Ramsey, Chuck, N.Y.J.	74	2964	79	40.1

AFC — INDIVIDUALS

	Punts	Yards	Long	Avg
McInally, Pat, Cin.	91	3919	65	43.1
Guy, Ray, Oak.	81	3462	69	42.7
Andrusyshyn, Zenon, K.C.	79	3247	61	41.1
Roberts, George, Mia.	81	3263	59	40.3
Ramsey, Chuck, N.Y.J.	74	2964	79	40.1
Colquitt, Craig, Pitt.	66	2642	58	40.0
Evans, Johnny, Clev.	79	3089	65	39.1
Parsley, Cliff, Hou.	91	3539	59	38.9
Jackson, Rusty, Buff.	87	3373	70	38.8
Lee, David, Balt.	92	3513	67	38.2
West, Jeff, S.D.	73	2720	59	37.3
Weaver, Herman, Sea.	66	2440	59	37.0

	Net Punts	Yards	Long	Avg
Skladany, Tom, Det.	86	3654	63	42.5
Jennings, Dave, N.Y.G.	95	3995	68	42.1
Blanchard, Tom, N.O.	84	3532	61	42.0
Green, Dave, T.B.	100	4092	61	40.9
White, Danny, Dall.	76	3076	56	40.5
Bragg, Mike, Wash.	103	4056	56	39.4
Coleman, Greg, Minn.	51	1991	61	39.0
James, John, Atl.	109	4227	57	38.8
Little, Steve, St.L.	46	1749	54	38.0
Connell, Mike, S.F.	96	3583	59	37.3

PUNT RETURNS

INDIVIDUAL CHAMPION
AFC: 13.7 (Yard Average)   Rick Upchurch, Denver (36 Returns; 493 Yards)
NFC: 11.9 (Yard Average)   Jackie Wallace, Los Angeles (52 Returns; 618 Yards)

YARDAGE
NFC: 618   Jackie Wallace, Los Angeles
AFC: 493   Rick Upchurch, Denver

RETURNS
NFC: 52   Jackie Wallace, Los Angeles
AFC: 47   Neal Colzie, Oakland

LONGEST
AFC: 82 (Yards)   Bruce Harper, New York Jets vs Buffalo, October 8 (TD); Keith Moody, Buffalo vs Houston, October 15 (TD)
NFC: 80 (Yards)   Tony Green, Washington vs Philadelphia, September 10 (TD)

TOUCHDOWNS

AFC: Bruce Harper, New York Jets vs Buffalo, October 8 (82 Yards); Keith Moody, Buffalo vs Houston, October 15 (82 Yards); Rick Upchurch, Denver vs San Diego, September 17 (75 Yards)

NFC: Tony Green, Washington vs Philadelphia, September 10 (80 Yards); Willard Harrell, St. Louis vs Washington, November 19 (70 Yards); Wally Henry, Philadelphia vs Los Angeles, September 3 (57 Yards); Steve Schubert, Chicago vs Washington, December 16 (73 Yards)

TEAM CHAMPION

AFC: 12.5 (Yard Average) New York Jets (33 Returns; 413 Yards)

NFC: 10.6 (Yard Average) Los Angeles (67 Returns; 711 Yards)

TOP TEN PUNT RETURNERS

	No	FC	Yards	Avg	Long	TD
Upchurch, Rick, Den. ...	36	2	493	13.7	t75	1
Moody, Keith, Buff.	19	5	240	12.6	t82	1
Harper, Bruce, N.Y.J. ...	30	4	378	12.6	t82	1
Wallace, Jackie, L.A. ...	52	5	618	11.9	58	0
Payton, Eddie, K.C.	32	2	364	11.4	39	0
Fuller, Mike, S.D.	39	10	436	11.2	34	0
Green, Tony, Wash.	42	13	443	10.5	t80	1
Morgan, Stanley, N.E. ..	32	5	335	10.5	48	0
Thompson, Jesse, Det. .	16	2	161	10.1	35	0
Harrell, Willard, St.L. ...	21	6	196	9.3	t70	1

Leader based on average return, minimum 16 returns

AFC — INDIVIDUALS

	No	FC	Yards	Avg	Long	TD
Upchurch, Rick, Den. ...	36	2	493	13.7	t75	1
Moody, Keith, Buff.	19	5	240	12.6	t82	1
Harper, Bruce, N.Y.J. ...	30	4	378	12.6	t82	1

Payton, Eddie, K.C.	32	2	364	11.4	39	0
Fuller, Mike, S.D.	39	10	436	11.2	34	0
Morgan, Stanley, N.E. ..	32	5	335	10.5	48	0
Coleman, Ronnie, Hou. .	16	1	142	8.9	32	0
Crawford, Rufus, Sea. ..	34	4	284	8.4	22	0
Cefalo, Jimmy, Mia.	28	8	232	8.3	26	0
Wright, Keith, Clev.	37	16	288	7.8	42	0

NFC — INDIVIDUALS

	No	FC	Yards	Avg	Long	TD
Wallace, Jackie, L.A. ...	52	5	618	11.9	58	0
Green, Tony, Wash.	42	13	443	10.5	t80	1
Thompson, Jesse, Det. .	16	2	161	10.1	35	0
Harrell, Willard, St.L. ...	21	6	196	9.3	t70	1
Odom, Steve, G.B. ...	33	7	298	9.0	48	0
Reece, Danny, T.B.	44	3	393	8.9	50	0
Schubert, Steve, Chi. ...	27	21	229	8.5	t73	1
Ryckman, Billy, Atl.	28	18	227	8.1	38	0
Johnson, Butch, Dall. ...	51	12	401	7.9	23	0
Leonard, Tony, S.F.-Det.	18	5	140	7.8	24	0

KICKOFF RETURNS

INDIVIDUAL CHAMPION
NFC: 27.1 (Yard Average) Steve Odom, Green Bay (25 Returns; 677 Yards)

AFC: 26.3 (Yard Average) Keith Wright, Cleveland (30 Returns; 789 Yards)

YARDAGE
AFC: 1280 Bruce Harper, New York Jets
NFC: 870 Tony Green, Washington

RETURNS

AFC: 55 Bruce Harper, New York Jets
NFC: 40 Kevin Miller, Minnesota

LONGEST

AFC: 102 (Yards) Curtis Brown, Buffalo vs Baltimore, September 24 (TD)
NFC: 100 (Yards) Dennis Pearson, Atlanta vs St. Louis, December 17 (TD)

TOUCHDOWNS

AFC: Larry Anderson, Pittsburgh vs Cleveland, October 15 (95 Yards); Curtis Brown, Buffalo vs Baltimore, September 24 (102 Yards); Joe Washington, Baltimore vs New England, September 18 (90 Yards)
NFC: Tony Green, Washington vs St. Louis, September 17 (99 Yards); Steve Odom, Green Bay vs Seattle, October 15 (95 Yards); Dennis Pearson, Atlanta vs St. Louis, December 17 (100 Yards); Dave Williams, San Francisco vs Los Angeles, November 19 (89 Yards)

TEAM CHAMPION

AFC: 23.9 (Yard Average) Kansas City (61 Returns; 1456 Yards)
NFC: 23.3 (Yard Average) Washington (58 Returns; 1352 Yards)

TOP TEN KICKOFF RETURNERS

	No	Yards	Avg	Long	TD
Odom, Steve, G.B.	25	677	27.1	t95	1
Pearson, Dennis, Atl.	25	662	26.5	t100	1
Wright, Keith, Clev.	30	789	26.3	86	0
Washington, Joe, Balt.	19	499	26.3	t90	1
Owens, Artie, S.D.	20	524	26.2	77	0
Payton, Eddie, K.C.	30	775	25.8	66	0
Green, Tony, Wash.	34	870	25.6	t99	1
Brown, Curtis, Buff.	17	428	25.2	t102	1
Anderson, Larry, Pitt.	37	930	25.1	t95	1
Dirden, Johnnie, Hou.	32	780	24.4	60	0

AFC — INDIVIDUALS

	No	Yards	Avg	Long	TD
Wright, Keith, Clev.	30	789	26.30	86	0
Washington, Joe, Balt.	19	499	26.26	t90	1
Owens, Artie, S.D.	20	524	26.2	77	0
Payton, Eddie, K.C.	30	775	25.8	66	0
Brown, Curtis, Buff.	17	428	25.2	t102	1
Anderson, Larry, Pitt.	37	930	25.1	t95	1
Dirden, Johnnie, Hou.	32	780	24.4	60	0
Hunter, Al, Sea.	16	385	24.1	38	0
Crawford, Rufus, Sea.	35	829	23.7	36	0
Clayborn, Raymond, N.E.	27	636	23.6	60	0

NFC — INDIVIDUALS

	No	Yards	Avg	Long	TD
Odom, Steve, G.B.	25	677	27.1	t95	1
Pearson, Dennis, Atl.	25	662	26.5	t100	1
Green, Tony, Wash.	34	870	25.6	t99	1
Chandler, Wes, N.O.	32	760	23.8	38	0
Ragsdale, George, T.B.	24	555	23.1	46	0
Mauti, Richard, N.O.	17	388	22.8	39	0
Baschnagel, Brian, Chi.	20	455	22.8	36	0
Williams, Dave, S.F.	34	745	21.9	t89	1
Latin, Jerry, St.L.-L.A.	24	515	21.5	41	0
Hofer, Paul, S.F.	18	386	21.4	40	0
Miller, Kevin, Minn. ..,......	40	854	21.4	38	0